First published in 2018 in Norwegian by Magikon forlag, Fjellveien 48A, N-1410 Kolbotn,
Norway. The right of Kristin Roskifte to be identified as the author and illustrator of this
work has been asserted by them in accordance with the Copyright, Designs and Patents Act,
1988 (United Kingdom).

First Published in 2020 in English by Wide Eyed Editions, an imprint of The Quarto Group
400 First Avenue North, Suite 400, Minneapolis, MN 55401, USA.
T (612) 344-8100 F (612) 344-8692 www.QuartoKnows.com

ISBN 978-0-7112-4524-2

The illustrations were created digitally.
Set in DIN

Published by Katie Cotton and Georgia Amson-Bradshaw
Translated by Siân Mackie
Edited by Lucy Brownridge
Production by Dawn Cameron

Manufactured in China RD112019

9 8 7 6 5 4 3 2 1

KRISTIN
ROSKIFTE

EVERYBODY
COUNTS

WIDE EYED EDITIONS

No one.

0

1

One person. He is lying in bed counting his heartbeats.
He wonders how many people are looking at the same stars right now.

Two people in the forest.
One of them says something the other will remember for the rest of his life.

2

3

Three people on a podium.
Two of them are thrilled to be in the top three.

Four people in a band. One of them is a twin. One of them is thinking about her daughter's birthday present. One of them will be injured soon.

5

Five people in a family. Three of them love reading.
One of them is secretly in love.

Six people in an elevator.
One of them is scared he's missing out. Two of them feel lonely.

6

7

Seven people in a police line-up.
Four of them have never done anything wrong.
All of them are scared they'll be singled out.

8

Eight people in a P.E. class. All of them are worried they'll be picked last for dodgeball.
One of them is looking forward to his sister's birthday party.

Nine people standing in line. Two of them have important decisions to make. One of them is about to be disappointed. One of them is looking forward to going to the movies with her son.

9

10

Ten people in a hair salon. One of them is going to a party.
One of them is going on a long trip. One of them has a business idea.

Eleven people on a soccer team.
Ten of them like playing soccer. One of them dreads going to school.

11

12 Twelve people at a birthday party. Two of them are thinking about how time flies.
One of them wishes her own birthday were sooner.

Thirteen people at a life-drawing class. Twelve of them forget everything else while they draw. One of them will soon become a father for the first time.

13

14

Fourteen people on a rollercoaster.
Eight of them are having a blast. One of them will never do it again.

Fifteen people at a funeral.
Thirteen of them are grieving. Two of them will soon run a marathon.

15

16 Sixteen people gardening in the backyard. One of them is annoyed at the people not participating. One of them loves seeing things grow. One of them does a headstand for fifteen minutes every day.

Seventeen people in the emergency room. One of them hopes to recover before the costume parade. Nine of them are frustrated they have to wait so long. One of them loses something.

17

18   Eighteen people in a library. One of them is wondering how many stories the library contains. Two of them find something more between the books.

WANTED

LAWYER
FORTUNE TELLER
AUDITOR
PSYCHOLOGIST
INTERIOR ARCHITECT
CLIMATOLOGIST
OPHTHALMOLOGIST
PRIVATE DETECTIVE
TOWN PLANNER
ARTIST

NEWS •HOT DOGS
•MAGAZINES

MISSING

Nineteen people in an office building. Ten of them work there.
One of them has a new assignment. One of them is told that the future looks dark.

19

20

Twenty people in a school history class. One of them is thinking about all the people who've lived before us. One of them is thinking about a lost teddy. One of them is dreading soccer training. One of them will become president.

Twenty-one people playing hide and seek. One of them is laughing too loudly. One of them is practicing doing a handstand. One of them will not be found before bedtime.

21

22 Twenty-two people in an apartment building.
Two of them have done something illegal. One of them works in a prison.
One of them is an obsessive collector. One of them hasn't left the apartment in eight years.

Twenty-three people in a prison. Eighteen of them have committed a crime.
All of them long to get out. One of them will escape with help from his wife.

23

24

Twenty-four people at a flea market.
One of them finds a missing teddy bear. One of them buys something
she doesn't need. Two of them buy things to use to make costumes.

Twenty-five people at a costume parade.
Twenty-four of them have dressed up as something that interests them.
Two of them forget how shy they are normally. One of them isn't dressed up.

25

26 Twenty-six people in a supermarket. One of them is stealing.
One of them gets inspired. Two of them are buying ingredients for a cake.

Twenty-seven people at an art exhibition. One of them is the artist.
One of them is blown away by the art. Two of them found each other at the library.

27

28 Twenty-eight people at a baking competition. The ten best bakers win cinema tickets. The winner receives two plane tickets to any destination.

Twenty-nine people in a club for people who only wear pink. One of them is thinking about canceling their membership. One of them got lost on their way to a workshop for people who are afraid of flying. One of them is a taxi driver.

29

30

Thirty people in a park. One of them is doing his first ever handstand.
Two of them have never visited a park before.
No one sees a crime being committed.

45 Forty-five people in traffic. Two of them are on the run. One of them is doing something very dangerous. One of them is dreaming of a bigger car.

50 Fifty people in a mall. One of them has great ambitions.
One of them is worrying about a disappointed customer.
Two of them are planning an important event.

60

Sixty people at a wedding. One of them catches the
bridal bouquet. One of them wants to be somewhere else.

Sixty-five people at a twin festival. Two of them have never been to a twin festival before. Three of them are not twins. Four of them fall in love.

65

75 Seventy-five people running a marathon. One of them has won the lottery and is only running because he's happy. Two of them are sisters but don't know about each other. One of them likes going to strangers' weddings and funerals.

85 Eighty-five people at the movie theater. The movie makes one of them see the world in a new light. Three of them think it's boring. One of them will watch the movie again in eighty-two years.

Ninety people at an award ceremony for artists. Five of them receive prizes.
Forty of them are jealous. One of them is happy to be alive.

90

100 A hundred people in a schoolyard. One of them will soon fall and get hurt.
One of them will develop a vaccine that saves millions of lives.

DE[

ATHENS	09[
LONDON	09[
SEOUL	09[
MADRID	09[
ESBJERG	09[
TOKYO	09[
LULEÅ	10[
ESKILSTUNA	10[

135 A hundred and thirty-five people at an airport. Nineteen of them are homesick. One of them is about to miss the flight. One of them is meeting their family for the first time. One of them doesn't want to be leaving, and won't be coming back.

ARTURES

2	LIMA	1020	1
3	EDINBURGH	1025	4
4	AMSTERDAM	1030	2
1	MEXICO CITY	1035	5
2	NEW YORK	1045	3
5	EVENES	1050	2
3	LANZAROTE	1100	1
2	ROTTERDAM	1110	3

Two hundred people on a beach.
One of them has read that there are as many stars
in the universe as there are grains of sand on Earth.
Two of them are panicking because they can't see their children.

200

400

Four hundred people at a demonstration.
One of them wants to learn to read. One of them needs important surgery.
One of them wants a telescope. One of them dreams of finding a best friend.
All of them want a better world.

1,000

A thousand people watch a large comet that won't pass close to Earth for another 2,533 years. Many of them wonder whether there is life on other planets. None of them knows for sure what the meaning of life is.

7,500,000,000

Seven and a half billion people on the same planet.
Every single one of them has their own unique story.
Everybody counts. One of them is you!

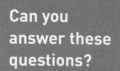

Can you answer these questions?

Where is he doing something dangerous?

What kind of job and hobby does he have?

Whose legs are these?

What will she regret?

What is her favourite sauce?

What is she an expert in?

What makes him happy?

What is she very interested in?

Who is driving this car?

Who are you?

Who knows the most about you?

Where was the horn bought?

What happened to the teddy?

What type of store does he own?

Who has this tattoo?

Where does she work?

Who is she married to?

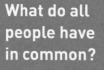
What kind of job does she have?

What does she teach?

What do all people have in common?

Whose is this wheelchair?

How is her hair causing problems?

What is she?

Who bought this picture at the art exhibition?

Whose dads are they?

Where does she work?

Does he survive?

Where was this selfie taken?

Where did they meet each other?

What is she buying at the jumble sale?

Where can you find her?

What is changing in her life?

Where can you find him?

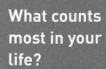
What do you think he is dreaming of?

What counts most in your life?

Where was this selfie taken?

Who do you think kissed him?

Is the world big or small?

How did his wife get plane tickets?

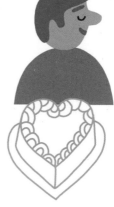
Where does he work?

Why do you think they are receiving a prize?

Where is she being robbed?

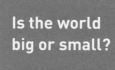
Who finds this and takes it home?

Where is he?

Why has he baked a heart-shaped cake?

Who is he waiting for?

What is her choice of costume?

Who has lost this?

Why is he flying up into the air?

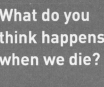
What do you think happens when we die?

Why is she dressed as a heart?

Where is he meeting an old friend?

Where can you find her?

Where was this selfie taken?

What does she do when she is not at strangers' weddings and funerals?

Why is she protesting?

Whose great-great-grandmother is this?

How many people have this book on the beach?

Where can you find her?

Where can you find him?

Have you seen this key?

What has he bought?

Does everyone share the same truth?

What is he overcoming a fear of?

Is there life on other planets?

What is she selling?

Where can you find him?

How old is he?

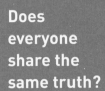
What is happening with him?

Where does he live?

Why is it strange he is wearing clothes?

In which two places does he fall asleep?

What is he missing?

What does she want to buy?

Where was this selfie taken?

Where would you find her?

Where is he relaxing?

Is there a baby in the stroller?

Why is she worried?

How much do we really know about each other?

Where does he work?

Who is this when not in costume?

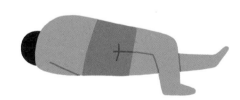
Why is he upset?

These eyes can be found in all the pictures – can you find them?

What do you think the meaning of life is?

Who is his partner?

What kind of job do you think she has?

What is outside of the universe?

She has three cousins. Who are they?

Where was this selfie taken?

Who took this picture?

Where can you find her?

SECRETS AND ANSWERS

1. The little boy is called Thomas. The stick on the floor is from the forest. A birthday card on the floor tells us he is eight. The globe is his favourite thing.

2. They have picked some mushrooms and put them in the basket. Thomas asks his dad what he thinks the meaning of life is. His dad says that right now it is spending time together in the woods.

3. The boy in second place is less satisfied with his efforts than Thomas is.

4. The guitarist is Thomas' mom. The trumpeter ends up in the hospital. The drummer is a twin.

5. All three kids love reading. Thomas is secretly in love. On the wall behind the family you can see some of the family history, including photos of the great-great-grandmother, an old family dog and their dad's childhood home.

6. The man with a phone is scared of missing something. The two who feel lonely are the man with red hair and blue sweater, and the woman in red sweater and pink skirt. They want to find someone to share their lives with but find it hard to meet new people.

7. All seven fit the same description, but still look very different. Number seven ends up in prison, but is he the guilty one? Number six often makes mistakes, here he has turned the sign upside down.

8. Thomas is looking forward to his big sister's birthday.

9. The woman with a purse and phone is going to the cinema with her son later. The woman with red sweater and long, brown hair is about to get a disappointing haircut. The woman in green is going to judge a baking competition. The woman in a purple dress has just found out she's having a baby.

10. The man at the sink is going to fly to Mexico. The man with a plaid shirt gets an idea to start a plant rental business. The woman with purple hair will get her roots dyed in time for her niece's birthday party. The woman with the pink jacket is a psychologist. The man waiting to pay is an auditor.

11. The goalkeeper dreads going to school.

12. The grandmother in blue glasses thinks that time goes too fast. She still remembers when she turned 12. The cousin in a spotty dress wishes it were her own birthday.

13. The man with purple pants will soon become a dad for the first time. The life model thinks about what to have for dinner.

14. The dad in the third carriage will never ride a roller coaster again.

15. The great-grandfather who was at the party has passed away at 94 years old. The two who aren't grieving are the priest and the woman behind him. She likes going to strangers' funerals and weddings!

16. The man in green is annoyed that there is someone who isn't helping. Thomas' aunt and cousin from the birthday party are there. The woman with a wheelbarrow does a headstand every day.

17. The man at the desk of the emergency room was also gardening in the backyard. The woman in purple dress is worried. Thomas has a fever and forgets his teddy. He is afraid that he will miss the fancy dress parade he is looking forward to. We will see later in the book if the man on the stretcher survives.

18. The two who felt lonely in the lift discover each other through the bookshelf. The woman with pink shoes borrows a book about escaping. The man who didn't help with the gardening uses a wheelchair. Who is the person with yellow pants and red shoes?

19. The auditor has bad news for the angry dad. The detective is hired to look for the lost teddy. She is also looking for the wanted man on the poster who is with his lawyer on the floor above. He is near the detective many times without her noticing him.

20. The kids have been asked to draw the Big Bang. The girl with the pink bow is the daughter of the angry dad. Her parents are divorced, she lives with her mom. The girl with spotty sweater is Thomas' girlfriend. The boy in the green sweater is dreading football training.

21. The boy at the top right isn't found before bedtime. The boy with striped sweater is practicing standing on his hands to impress his dad. The laundry belongs to the tall, thin woman on the drawing course, and her husband. The angry dad lives in the front house.

22. The man on the fifth floor, to the right, runs a flower shop and loves peace and quiet. The trumpet player from the band lives in the apartment next door. Once they started fighting and the trumpeter had to go to the emergency room! Thomas' aunt and cousin live on the floor below. The

mother of the girl with the pink ribbon in her hair is an obsessive collector of cushions. The person behind the roller blind has not been out of the apartment for eight years. The detective lives above the woman who stands on her head every day. The man who uses a wheelchair lives on the first floor.

23. Thomas' aunt works in prison and is looking forward to the end of the day. One of the inmates has been in prison for eight years. The man on the far left of the fourth floor will get help from his wife to escape. The woman in the upper right is a twin. The woman at the bottom left regrets the crime she committed. The man in the basement regrets nothing.

24. The woman with a pink skirt finds something that can be used in a teapot costume. The woman in green thinks that she can use the star for a unicorn costume for the kids. Thomas sees a globe that is different from his and thinks it is strange that the world can be seen in different ways. The woman who collects cushions finds another cushion. Thomas' mom finds the teddy. The wife of the man in prison finds a hacksaw and has an idea. The angry dad has given away the vase from his window.

25. The tall, thin woman from the drawing class is dressed as a pencil. The people dressed as the fruit basket and flamingo decide to wear their costumes forever. Thomas is dressed as the universe, his sister as ice cream, the little brother as a gift, and the dad as a tree. The woman from the lift and the library is in love and is dressed like a heart. The artist is dressed as the *Mona Lisa*. The woman dressed as a selfie takes selfies as often as she can. Now she's taking a selfie selfie! The man with the plant business is dressed up as a cactus. He is dangerously close to the balloon seller, who is not wearing a costume.

26. If you count the people, you can work out that there is no baby in the stroller. The man with the pram is stealing. The artist is inspired by the store shelves that form beautiful patterns. The life model is deciding what to make for dinner. The woman who collects cushions is bent down in the freezer. The lonely man from the lift is buying a meal for one. The pregnant woman is tired. The woman who dressed as a ketchup bottle at the fancy dress parade buys ketchup. The wife of the man in prison buys ingredients for a cake and so does Thomas.

27. Thomas is having an art experience that will prove crucial to his choice of career. The artist, who is wearing a yellow jacket and black ponytail, is pleased with the turn out. The two who met at the library are enjoying each other's company. The woman with sunglasses will soon be a victim of theft. The person with yellow pants and red shoes appears to the left of the picture. Who could it be?